WITCHCRAFT IN IRELAND

By the same author:
Irish Ghost Stories

Witchcraft in Ireland

BY PATRICK F. BYRNE

Mercier Press
Cork

© *Patrick F. Byrne, 1967*

Reprinted 1969
Reprinted 1973
Reprinted 1975

Mercier Press
Cork
www.mercierpress.ie
Moved to Digital Print-on-Demand in 2025

For Diarmuid

Ireland has been singularly free from witch prosecutions, and with the rarest exceptions – chiefly, if not solely, the famous Dame Alice Kyteler case of 1324 – the few trials recorded are of the 17th century and engineered by the Protestant party. The reason for this exemption is plain. Until the stranger forced his way into Ireland, heresy had no foothold there. That the Irish firmly believed in witches, we know, but the devil's claws were finely clipped. –

Dr. Montague Summers in *The History of Witchcraft*.

ACKNOWLEDGEMENTS

I wish to thank Mr. John J. Finegan for his helpful comments on reading the manuscript; Mr. David O. Watson of Belfast for his information about modern witchcraft in the North, and last, but not least, my wife for her typing and other help. I am also indebted to the authors, both living and dead, of the books listed in the bibliography at the end.

The first four lines of the poem, *The Host of the Air,* and the extracts from *Irish Fairy Tales and Folk Tales* appear by kind permission of Mr. M. B. Yeats and Messrs Macmillan & Co. Ltd. I would also like to thank the staffs of the National Library and of Trinity College Library for their never failing help and courtesy at all times.

CONTENTS

Acknowledgements
Introduction 11
1. Witchcraft in Early Irish Literature 13
2. Dame Alice Kyteler – (the 14th Century) . . 18
3. Florence Newton (The Witch of Youghal) and other Happenings of the 17th Century . 28
4. Island Magee and The Hell Fire Club – (the 18th Century) 38
5. Carrickfergus – (the 19th Century) 51
6. The Clonmel Burning – (the 19th Century) . 56
7. The Witch in Folklore 69
Postscript 75
Bibliography 76

INTRODUCTION

Apart from the famous Dame Alice Kyteler affair in the early part of the 14th century there were very few, of what one might call, sensational witchcraft cases recorded in Ireland. The majority of trials for witchcraft took place in the country in the 16th and 17th centuries when Puritanism was in the ascendant. Regrettably, many of these were not recorded, and only a few have come down to us.

In his rare book on Irish witches published in 1913 St. John Seymour said that in Ireland Catholics were always associated with the fairies and Protestants with witches. He added that the country's remoteness, and the fact that it was not occupied by the Romans had something to do with not having a tradition of witches in Ireland.

If there had been no Anglo-Norman invasion, he said, Ireland might have imbibed the witchcraft spirit, and blended it with older beliefs. The invasion prevented the growth and spread of witchcraft in Ireland. The turmoil and clash of war gave the people other things to think about, and there was a lack of literature on the subject.

The famous scholar, Giraldus Cambrensis, who visited Ireland in the 12th century, said that Irish witches could turn wisps of hay or straw into red-coloured pigs, which they dishonestly sold in the market, but which resumed their proper shape when crossing running water. To prevent this, he stated that the Irish Parliament passed an Act forbidding the purchase of red swine. This is the earliest reference to the modern-type witch's activities in Ireland.

One accusation of witchcraft could easily be explained. As the country was occupied by the English, it is almost certain that under cover of darkness the native Irish crept down from the hills, maimed and milked cattle, or did other damage to the invaders, such as the Underground did in the Nazi-occupied countries of Europe during the last War. In such an instance some innocent old woman could easily be accused of witchcraft.

In the following pages I have tried to give all known cases of witchcraft from pre-christian times, featuring the Dame Kyteler case, the Witch of Youghal (17th century), the Island Magee case in the 18th century, and ending with the Clonmel witch burning in the late 19th century, the last recorded case in Ireland.

CHAPTER 1

WITCHCRAFT IN EARLY IRISH LITERATURE

Of course, one could say that it all started in ancient Ireland for according to the *Annals of Clonmacnoise* the Tuatha de Danaan princes ruling the country around the year 2,000 B.C. were master sorcerers with immense powers. Their three fierce goddesses were witch-types in every sense. They were usually referred to as Badhb (scald-crow), Macha and Morrigan (Queen of Phantoms).

They were represented as creatures of ill-omen and of horrible appearance, who foretold death and disaster, brooded over battlefields, stimulated strife and slaughter, and revelled in the pain and desolation which followed warfare. Sir Plunket Barton in his book *Links Between Ireland and Shakespeare* said they were probably the inspiration for the Three Witches in *Macbeth*.

The Morrigan was said to live in the Cave of Cruachan in Connacht, one-time called the Hell's Gate of Ireland. From it were said to issue a flock of white birds that withered everything up with their breath, and hordes of pigs which devasted the surrounding country side. In the *Tain Bo Cuailgne,* the Morrigan meets Cuchullain and warns of his death at the Pillar Stone, and breaks his chariot to try and stop him from going into battle.

An early account of a witch in Irish history is given by Standish O'Grady in his *Silva Gadelica* (1892) under the title, *The Cave of Keshcorran*. It tells how Finn Mac Cumhaill, when out hunting with Conan Mael trespassed on the lands of a Tuatha de Danaan magician named Conaran, who was so annoyed by this that he sent his three daughters to take vengeance on Finn. They went into a cave and changed their appearance into that of hideous old hags. As Finn and each member of the Fianna went into the cave they were enmeshed in the yarn the hags were spinning and made prisoner. The hags then changed back into warrior-women and were about to massacre their prisoners when Goll Mac Morna comes to the rescue and kills them instead.

THE EVIL EYE

A terrifying sort of male witch was Balor of the Evil Eye – the Gaelic version of the Cyclops. Balor had one huge eye in the centre of his forehead, and it was never opened except on a battlefield when it took four men to lift the eyelid. If an army looked at the eye it was rendered powerless. Balor was killed by the Celtic God, Lugh, who walked around the monster, chanting a dirge. Hearing the sound Balor's curiosity was too much for him, and ordered his eyelid to be lifted. Immediately, Lugh shot a sling stone through the eye and cut off his head. Lughnasa, the Celtic Autumn Festival of the First Fruits was named after Lugh.

THE CAILLEACH BEARA

> I am the Woman of Beare.
> Foul am I that was fair,
> Good embroidered smocks I had,
> Now in rags am hardly clad.

The Cailleach Beara, or Old Woman of Beare, the

peninsula in West Munster is mentioned by Padraic Pearse in his poem *Mise Eire*. She figures in Scottish as well as Irish folk tales. Mountains, lakes and islands in Ireland are named after her, and cairns are said to be stones which fell from her apron.

A note in the mediaeval *Book of Lecan* says the Cailleach was of the Corca Duibhne: 'This is why she was called the Old Woman of Beare: she had 50 foster children in Beare. She passed into seven periods of youth; so that every husband used to pass from her to death of old age, and so that her grandchildren and great grand-children were people and races.'

Pearse's comparison of Ireland with the Cailleach was an apt one in view of the fact that she renewed her youth over and over again.

The Kerry seanchaidhe, Sean O Conaill told Dr. Seamus O Duilearga many stories about the Hag of Beare which are to be found in Dr. O Duilearga's large and entertaining volume, *Leabhar Sheain I Chonaill*. He said she was one of three sisters who lived long ago in Co. Kerry. One lived in Dingle, another in Bolus and the third in Beare. They were all known to be witches, and were not well off, but the poorest of all was the Witch of Beare.

One of his stories tells how one day the Witch of Bolus was salting a hundredweight of butter in her house when she heard a loud cry outside. She said to her husband: 'I recognise that cry. My sister is calling from Beare and that means there must be something wrong.' The husband went out and said there was a white cow in the cornfield on the north-east of the house. This showed how powerful was the eyesight of the Witch of Beare.

The Witch of Dingle, said Sean O Conaill, lived to be more than 300 years old. 'It became known all over the nation that she was so old, and crowds came from far away places to try and find out why she lived so long. The only information she would give them was that she had always covered the top of her head, had never touched the earth with the soles of her feet, and never slept unless she felt sleepy.

THE CHILDREN OF LIR

The Fate of the Children of Lir, one of the Three Sorrows of Story-telling of the Gael contains a witch motif on the same style as the modern *Snow White* one.

The De Danaan princes, after defeating the Firbolgs at the Battle of Taiteann, elected Bove Dearg, son of the Dagda as their King. One of those angered by the decision was Lir of Shee Finnaha, but later goodwill was restored between them when Bove Dearg gave his beautiful daughter, Eve to Lir in marriage. She bore him twins – a daughter and a son, named Finola and Aedh. A year or so later she again brought forth twins, named Fiachra and Conn, but died giving them birth.

Lir was grief-stricken, but after a while Bove Dearg offered him his second daughter, Eva, in marriage. They were espoused and she took over the care of the four little children. As they grew both Lir and Bove Dearg grew more and more fond of the children, and Eva got jealous of this as time went on.

One day she brought the children in her chariot to visit her father's palace. On the way she asked the servants to kill them. Horrified, they refused. She took a sword to commit the foul deed herself, but her womanly instinct restrained her. She then drove to the shore of Lake Derravarragh (Co. Westmeath).

She told the children to go and bathe, and when they had got into the clear water she struck them with a magic wand and they were turned into four beautiful snow-white swans.

She then told them their fate – they were to spend 300 years on Lake Derravaragh; 300 years on the Sea of Moyle between Ireland and Scotland and 300 years on Inis Glora (off Belmullet) in the Western Sea. The coming of St. Patrick and the ringing of the Christian bell would release them from their enchantment. The wicked stepmother relenting gave them two concessions – they were to retain their Gaelic speech and to be able to sing sweet music that would lull to sleep anyone who heard it.

Needless to remark Lir was overcome with great sorrow and anger when he heard what had befallen. He hastened to Bove Dearg's house where Eva had taken refuge, and when her father heard the story he struck her with his druidical wand and changed her into a demon of the air. 'She opened her wings, and flew with a scream upwards and away through the clouds; and she is still a demon of the air, and she shall be a demon of the air till the end of time.'

CHAPTER 2

DAME ALICE KYTELER (THE 14TH CENTURY)

The mediaeval residence, Dame Kyteler's house is one of Kilkenny's most historic relics. Dame Kyteler was of an Anglo-Norman family which had been living in Kilkenny for many years. The coffin-shaped tombstone of one of her ancestors is preserved in St. Mary's Church. The inscription is in Norman French and the lettering in Lombardic.

Dame Alice was said to have been very handsome, and had four husbands. They were, in order of sequence -- William Outlawe of Kilkenny, a banker; Adam le Blund of Callan; Richard de Valle (all of whom she is said to have poisoned) and Sir John le Poer, whom she is said to have deprived of his natural senses by philtres and incantations.

The Bishop of Ossory at the time was Richard de Ledrede, a Franciscan friar and English by birth. Hearing rumours of strange goings on he made a visitation of his diocese in 1324, and by means of an Inquisition, consisting of five Knights and several nobles found there was a band of heretical sorcerers in the city, headed by Dame Alice. The Inquisition drew up the following charges

1 – That the sorcerers had denied the faith of Christ absolutely for a year and a month, according as the object they desired to gain through sorcery was of greater or lesser importance. During this period they believed in none of the doctrines of the Church; did not adore the Body of Christ, nor hear Mass, nor make use of consecrated bread or holy water.

2 – They offered in sacrifice to demons living animals, which they dismembered, and then distributed at cross-roads to a certain evil spirit of low rank, named the Son of Art.

3 – They sought by their sorceries advice and responses from demons.

4 – In their nightly meetings they blasphemously imitated the power of the Church by fulminating sentence of ex-communication, with lighted candles, even against their own husbands.

5 – In order to arouse feelings of love or hatred or to inflict death or disease on the bodies of the faithful, they made use of powders, unguents, ointments and candles of fat, which were compounded as follows: they took the entrails of cocks sacrificed to demons, certain horrible worms, various unspecified herbs, dead men's nails the hair, brains and shreds of grave clothes of boys who were buried unbaptized, with other abominations, all of which were cooked, with various incantations, over a fire of oak logs in a vessel made out of the skull of a decapitated thief.

6 – The children of Dame Alice's first three husbands accused her before the Bishop of having killed their fathers by sorcery, and of having enchanted them so that they left all the wealth to her and her favourite son, William Outlawe, to the impoverishment of the other children. They said her present husband (Sir John le Poer) had been reduced to such condition by sorcery and powders that he had become terribly emaciated, his nails had dropped off and there was no hair on his body. He would have died had he not been warned by a maidservant, in consequence of which he forcibly possessed himself of his wife's keys and had opened some chests in which he found a sackful of horri-

ble and detestable things which he transmitted to the Bishop through the hands of two priests.

7 – The Dame had a certain demon, an incubus named Art or Robin, son of Art, who had carnal knowledge of her, and from whom she admitted she had received all her wealth. This incubus made its appearance under various forms sometimes as a cat, as a hairy black dog or in the likeness of a Negro (Aethiops), accompanied by two others who were large and taller than he, and of whom one carried an iron rod.

Another source said the sacrifice to evil spirits consisted of nine red cocks and nine peacock eyes. Dame Alice was also accused of having 'swept the streets of Kilkenny between compline and twilight, raking all the filth towards the doors of her son, William Outlawe, chanting:

> 'To the house of William my sonne,
> Hie all the wealth of Kilkenny town.'

BISHOP OF OSSORY

The Bishop of Ossory wrote to the Chancellor of Ireland, Roger Outlawe, Prior of the Preceptory of Kilmainham for the arrest of the people involved. William Outlawe immediately gathered his followers around him for protection, and appealed to the Chancellor (a near relative) and Sir Arnold le Poer, the Seneschal of Kilkenny, probably related to Dame Alice's last husband.

The Chancellor told the Bishop that a warrant for arrest could not be obtained until a public process of excommunication had been in force for 40 days, and Sir Arnold wrote asking that the case be withdrawn or ignored. Finding such obstacles in his way the Bishop took the matter into his own hand, and cited the Dame, who was in her son's house in Kilkenny to appear before him. She ignored the citation and fled.

The Bishop then cited her son William for heresy. Hearing this Sir Arnold came with William to the Priory of Kells, where De Ledrede was holding a visitation and besought him not to proceed further in the matter. The Bishop refused, and the following day, as he was continuing his visitation, he was met on the confines of the town by Stephen le Poer, bailiff of Overk, and a posse of armed men, by whom he was arrested under orders from Sir Arnold, and lodged in Kilkenny Jail.

This caused an uproar in the city. The place became subject to an interdict; the Bishop called for the Sacrament and it was brought to him in solemn procession by the Dean and Chapter. All the clergy flocked from every side to the prison to console the captive and feeling was roused to fever pitch by a Dominican who preached on the text, 'Blessed are they who are persecuted.' As a result things were relaxed for the Bishop, and free admission to the jail was granted to his friends and servants.

After 17 days had elapsed, and the day on which William Outlawe was to have appeared before the Bishop had passed, Sir Arnold, his end achieved, sent by the hand of his uncle, the Bishop of Leighlin (Miler de Poer), and the Seneschal of Kilkenny, a mandate to the Constable of the prison to liberate the Bishop, who refused to sneak out like a felon, but assumed his pontificals, and accompanied by all the clergy, and a throng of people, made his way solemnly to St. Canice's Cathedral where a 'Te Deum' was sung.

After this he again incited William Outlawe to appear before him, but before the day arrived, the Bishop was himself cited to answer in Dublin for placing the interdict on his diocese. He excused himself from attending on the plea that the road to the capital passed through the lands of Sir Arnold, and in consequence his life would be in danger.

SENESCHAL'S COURT

De Ledrede had been arrested by Le Poer's orders in Lent. On the Monday following the octave of Easter the Seneschal held his court in Kilkenny to which entrance was denied the bishop, but the latter, fully robed, and carrying the Sacrament in a golden monstrance, made his way into the courtroom, and 'ascending the tribunal, and reverently elevating the Body of Christ, sought from the Seneschal, Justiciary and bailiffs that hearing should be granted to him.'

There was a heated scene between the Seneschal and bishop, during which the former called the latter 'a vile rustic, interloping monk' and refused to hear his arguments or to afford him any assistance.

In the meantime, hiding away in the background, Dame Alice used her influence to have the bishop summoned to Dublin to answer for having excommunicated her, uncited, unadmonished and unconvicted of the crime of sorcery. The bishop attended to answer the charges and found the courts of the King and Archbishop against him to a man, but on putting his case he won the day. As a result Sir Arnold was humbled and sought pardon for the wrong he had done the bishop. This was granted, and in front of the assembled Council and prelates the two men exchanged the kiss of peace.

The bishop was now able to proceed with the delayed indictment. He asked the Chancellor to apprehend Dame Alice, and also directed the Vicar-General of the Archbishop of Dublin to cite her to respond on a certain day in Kilkenny before the bishop. But the quarry again escaped. Dame Alice fled from Dublin where she had been living, and (it is said) made her way to England where she spent the remainder of her days unmolested.

Her confederates were arrested and committed to prison. They were: – Robert of Bristol, a clerk, John Galrussyn, Ellen Galrussyn, Syssok Galrussyn, William Payn de Boly, Petronilla of Meath, her aunt Sarah, Alice, the wife of Henry Faber, Annota Lange and Eva de Drownestown. They were all close friends or retainers of Dame Alice.

When the bishop arrived in Kilkenny from Dublin he immediately went to interview the prisoners. They all at once admitted the charges, and even confessed to other crimes to which no charges had been made, and all said that Dame Alice was the leader.

On June 6 the bishop wrote to the Chancellor and the Treasurer, Walter de Islep, requesting them to order the Seneschal to put the prisoners in safe keeping for trial. But warrant was refused as William Outlawe was a relation of one and close friend of another, so eventually the bishop obtained the order through the Justiciary, who also consented to deal with the case when he arrived in Kilkenny.

ARMED IN CHURCH

William Outlawe was summoned to appear in St. Mary's Church. He arrived with a band of men, all armed to the teeth. The bishop, completely unaffected formally accused him of heresy, of favouring, receiving and defending heretics, as well as of usury, perjury, adultery, clericide and excommunications — 34 items in all were brought against him, and he was permitted to respond on the arrival of the Justiciary.

When the latter reached Kilkenny on July 2, accompanied by the Chancellor, the Treasurer and the King's Council, the bishop, in their presence, recited the charges against Dame Alice, and with common consent of the lawyers present described her to be a sorceress, magician and heretic, and demanded that she be handed over to the secular arm and have her good and chattels confiscated also.

On the day the bishop caused a great fire to be lit in the middle of the town in which he burnt the sackful of magical abominations which he had earlier received from Sir John le Poer.

After more trouble with William Outlawe (still backed by the Chancellor and Treasurer), the bishop finally brought him to submission on his bended knees. By way of penance he was ordered to hear at least three Masses daily for the space of a year, to feed a certain number of poor people, and to cover with lead the chancel of St. Canice's Cathedral from the belfry eastward, as well as the chapel of the Blessed Virgin Mary. At first Outlawe agreed to this, but later refused, and was thrown into prison.

PETRONILLA'S FATE

Of the accomplices, Petronilla of Meath was made the scapegoat for her mistress. The bishop had her flogged six times after which she made the confession of magical practices which was expected of her. She admitted denial of the Faith, sacrificing to Robin, son of Art, and that she had caused certain women of her acquaintance to appear as if they had goat's horns.

She also confessed that at the suggestion of Dame Alice she had frequently consulted demons and received responses from them, and that she acted as a 'medium' (Mediatrix) between her and the said Robin. She declared that although she herself was mistress of the Black Art, yet she was as nothing in comparison with the Dame from whom she had learned all her knowledge, and that there was no-one in the world more skilful than she.

She also stated that William Outlawe deserved death as much as she, for he was privy to their sorceries, and for a year and a day had 'worn the devil's girdle around his body.'

When searching Dame Alice's house there was found 'a wafer of sacramental bread having the devil's name stamped on it instead of Jesus Christ, and a pipe of ointment wherewith she greased a staffe, upon which she ambled and galloped through thick and thin, when and in what name she listed.'

Petronilla was accordingly condemned to be burnt alive, and the execution took place with all due solemnity in Kilkenny on Sunday, November 3, 1324. This was the first instance of the penalty of death by fire being inflicted in Ireland for heresy. There is no official record of what happened the other prisoners, some may have later suffered Petronilla's fate for an anonymous report stated: –

'With regard to the other heretics and sorcerers who belonged to the pestilential society of Robin, son of Art, the order of the law being preserved, some of them were publicly burnt to death; others, confessing their crimes in the presence of all the people, in an upper garment are marked back and front with a cross after they had abjured their heresy which is the custom; others were solemnly whipped through the town and the market place; others were banished from the city and diocese; others who evaded the jurisdiction of the Church were excommunicated; while others again fled in fear and were never heard of after, and thus, by the authority of Holy Mother the Church and by the special grace of God, that most foul brood was scattered and destroyed.'

The bishop's next move was to accuse Sir Arnold le Poer of heresy and had him excommunicated and committed a prisoner to Dublin Castle. No one believed him guilty and Roger Outlawe, the Prior of Kilmainham, who was appointed Justiciary of Ireland in 1328 showed him kindness and treated him with humanity. This so enraged the bishop that he accused the Justiciary himself of heresy.

A select committee of clerics vindicated the orthodoxy of the latter, upon which he prepared a sumptuous banquet for his defenders. Le Poer died in prison the same year, 1331, before the matter was finally settled, and as he was under ban of excommunication his body lay unburied for a long period.

Ultimately the tables were turned with a vengeance. Bishop de Ledrede was himself accused of heresy by his Metropolitan, Alexander de Bicknor, upon which he appealed to the Holy See and set out in person for Avignon (where the Pope was living in exile). This involved a long absence from his diocese, he suffered much hardship, and had his property seized by the Crown.

In 1339 he regained the royal favour, but ten years later further accusations were brought to the King against him, and his property again seized. By 1356 the storm had blown over, he regained his episcopate and reigned undisturbed until his death in 1360. He was buried in the chancel of St. Canice's on the north side of the high altar. A recumbent effigy under a canopy is said to mark his last resting place.

Richard de Ledrede became a bishop almost at the same time as John XXII was elevated to the Papacy. This pope adopted a stern attitude to sorcery and the magical arts, and denounced such practices in his Bulls. This may have encouraged the Bishop of Ossory to search diligently for such practices in his diocese.

The Kyteler case was the only occasion on which the use of torture in connection with witchcraft was recorded in Ireland.

HERETICS BURNED

Another instance of death by fire was recorded in 1353 when two men were tried at Bunratty, Co. Clare by Roger Cradok, Bishop of Waterford, for holding heretical opinions (or for offering contumely to the Blessed Virgin) and were sentenced to be burned.

Witch trials were held again in Kilkenny in 1578 but the records unfortunately have been lost. In November of that year at sessions held by Lord Justice Drury and Sir Henry Fitton whose letter to the Privy Council stated: 'the jail being full we caused session immediately to be held. Thirty-six persons were executed, amongst them some good ones, a blackamoor and two witches by natural law, for that we find no law to try them by in the realm.' One wonders what the unfortunate Negro was doing in Kilkenny, and why he met his sad fate, and was he the Aethiops mentioned in the Kyteler charges.

A Statute against witchcraft was passed by the Irish Parliament in 1586 to bring the country's laws into line with England. The penalties mentioned were imprisonment and spells on the pillory and 'death as a felon' for second offence and of course confiscation of property. This law was never repealed.

CHAPTER 3

FLORENCE NEWTON (THE WITCH OF YOUGHAL) AND OTHER HAPPENINGS OF THE 17TH CENTURY

In the 17th century there was a colony of Puritans in the town of Youghal where a famous witch trial took place in 1661. On March 24 of that year an old woman, Florence Newton was committed to Youghal Prison for bewitching Mary Longdon, who gave evidence at the trial at Cork Assizes on the following September.

When Mary Longdon was sworn she was told to look at the prisoner and 'her countenance changed pale, and she was very fearful to look towards her, but at last she did, and being asked whether she knew her she said she did, and wished she never had.' Asked how long she had known her, she said for three or four years.'

Mary said that at Christmas Florence Newton came to her at the house of John Pyne in Youghal where she was employed as a servant and asked her to give her a piece of beef and Mary answered that she could not give away her Master's beef. Florence went away very angry and grumbling to herself.

About a week later when Mary was going to the well for water Florence came to her and violently kissed her saying - 'Mary, let us be friends; for I bear you no ill will, and I hope you bear me none.'

Mary went home and for a few days after she saw a woman with a veil over her face standing by her bedside, and beside the figure was a little old man in silk clothes, and this man whom she took to be a spirit, drew the veil off the woman's face and she knew it was Florence Newton. The spirit spoke to her, Mary said, and asked her to promise to follow his advice, and she could have anything she wanted. She said she would have nothing to do with him, 'for her trust was in the Lord.'

She said that within a month after Florence had kissed her, she suffered from sudden attacks of fits and trances, and three or four men could not hold her down. During her fits she vomited up needles, pins, horsenails, stubbs, wool and straw. Also that from time to time small stones fell upon her as she went from one room to another, hitting her on the head, shoulders and arms, vanishing when they fell to the ground.

This was seen by other people including her Master.

In her fits she cried out in pain saying she saw Florence Newton who stuck pins into her arms with so much force that a man found it hard to pull them out afterwards. Sometimes she was lifted out of the bed into another room; at other times she was lifted to the roof of the house and placed on a board between two beams. She also said she was put into a chest, and between the bed and the mat in her Master's chamber during the daytime.

She was always worse when the Mayor brought Florence Newton to her, and the fits became more violent. When Florence was committed to jail in Youghal she was better for a while, but when Florence was removed to Cork Jail she was as bad as before. When the Mayor of Youghal insisted that Florence be chained in her cell, Mary got well again and remained so afterwards.

Mary concluded her evidence by saying that she believed that the kiss Florence had given her had bewitched her.

When Mary had finished Florence Newton raised

up her manacled hands in the court in the girl's direction, as if she intended to strike at her and said 'Now she is down.' Immediately Mary fell to the ground like a stone and went into a most violent fit, biting her arms and shrieking to the amazement of onlookers, and continued to do so for a quarter of an hour.

She was taken from the court into a house where she was reported to have vomited up crooked pins, straws and wool in great proportion. At the same time Florence Newton was seen to be pinching her own hands and arms in the courthouse.

It was decided to bind Florence with chains and Mary became well again.

A witness, Nicolas Stout, was produced by the Attorney General, and he said he heard that witches could not properly repeat the Lord's Prayer. He had tried it out and she could not say it.

She was then asked to say it in court, and four times, after the words, 'Give us this day our daily bread,' she continually said 'As we forgive them,' leaving out altogether the words 'And forgive us our trespasses.' The court appointed someone to teach her the words, but she could not, or would not say them.

John Pyne said that in January, 1661 his serving maid Mary Longdon was troubled with small stones, as she had stated. Sometimes she had been reading a Bible, and he had seen it struck out of her hand into the middle of the room, immediately after which she was cast into a violent fit.

Nicholas Pyne said that on the second night after the witch had been in prison in March, he with Joseph Thompson, Roger Hawkins and others went to speak with her and she denied that she had bewitched the girl, but said that she had 'overlooked' her and that there was a big difference between overlooking and bewitching. She fell on her knees and prayed to God to forgive her if she had wronged the girl. Then she said there were others such as Mistress Halfpenny and Mistress Dodd in town that could do these things as well as she, and that it might be one of those who had done the girl wrong.

Towards evening the door of the prison shook and she got up and said: 'What are you doing here at this time of night?' There was a great noise as if someone with bolts and chains was running up and down the room. When questioned about this Florence denied saying anything, and also said that she neither heard nor saw anything unusual. Next day, however, she admitted asking the question and said the noise was caused by a spirit, and that it was her familiar in the shape of a greyhound.

Edward Perry then gave evidence and said that with Mr. Greatrix and Mr. Blackwall he went to Mary Longdon. Mr. Greatrix said he had read of a way to discover a witch, which he would practise.

They sent for the witch and put her on a stool and a shoemaker with a strong awl tried to stick it into the stool, but could not until the third time. Then they told her to get off the stool, but she said she was too tired and couldn't stir. The two of them pulled her off, and the shoemaker went to pull out his awl and it dropped into his hand with half an inch broken off the blade, and they all looked to find out where it had been stuck, but could find no place where any entry had been made by it.

Then they took another awl and put it into the girl's hand, and one of them took the girl's hand, and ran violently at the witch's hand with it, but could not enter it, though the awl was so bent that none of them could put it straight again. Then Mr. Blackwall took a lance and lanced one of the witch's hands an inch and a half long and a quarter of an inch deep, but it didn't bleed. Then he lanced the other hand and they both bled.

Mr. Wood, a Minister, being sworn, at the trial said having heard of the girl's fits and of the stones thrown at her he went along and found her in bed in a fit 'crying out against Newton, saying that she pricked and hurt her.' When she came to, she said that Newton had been standing by the bedside. They went out and brought in Florence Newton and on seeing her the girl cried out; when she went away the girl prayed, and when she was brought back gain the girl went into a fit and cried out that she was being strangled.

Richard Mayre, the Mayor of Youghal told the court how on March 24 he sent for Florence Newton, who denied the charges against her and accused Mistress Halfpenny and Mistress Dodd. When he caused a boat to be provided and said he would try the water experiment on the three of them Florence Newton confessed to 'overlooking.' The other two women utterly denied the charges, and said they were content to abide any trial.

They were brought to the girl, who said, 'No, no, they are honest women, but it is Mistress Newton that hurts me, and I believe she is not far off.' He further deposed that there were three Aldermen in Youghal whose children she had kissed, and he had heard them affirm that all the children died shortly afterwards.

BEWITCHED JAILER

While in Cork Prison Florence Newton was said to have bewitched one David Jones to death by kissing his hand through the grate of the prison, for which she was also indicted at Cork Assizes.

Eleanor Jones, the jailer's widow, giving evidence, told how her husband came home early in the morning and said: 'Where do thou think I have been all night?' She said she did not know and he replied – 'I and Frank Besely have been standing sentinel over the witch.'

He then told how the witch had kissed his hand and said there was a great pain in his arm, and that he was bewitched. All that night he was restless and ill and continued so for seven days. He complained that the pain had gone from his arm to his heart, and he kept crying out against Florence Newton, and about fourteen days later he died.

The other jailor, Francis Besely, then told how he and Jones, at the time aforementioned discussed the reports that Florence Newton had several familiars resorting to her in various shapes. Jones said he would watch one night to see if he could observe cats or other creatures go into her cell through the grate.

The two men went to the cell and Jones said to Florence that he heard she could not say the Lord's Prayer. She answered that she could, but said that her memory was bad through old age. Then he began to teach it to her, but she would not, or could not repeat it no matter how many times he said it.

A while later she called out to Jones: 'David, I can say the Lord's Prayer now.' Jones went to the grate and she began to say the Lord's Prayer, but could not say 'Forgive us our trespasses' and Jones again taught her.

She then said she desired to kiss his hand and he gave it to her through the grate and she did so. He later heard that Jones was ill and went to see him.

Jones told him that the hag had him by the hand and was pulling off his arm.

The Mr. Greatrix was Valentine Greatrakes, the famous healer or 'stroker' who was born in 1629 and died in 1683. He joined the Puritan Army and when it was disbanded in 1656 became a country magistrate. At the Restoration in 1660 he was deprived of his offices.

In 1662 he found he had a 'Gift' when he cured a boy by stroking him. His fame spread and people came from all parts of England and Ireland to be cured. The form he used was: – 'God Almighty heal thee for his Mercy's sake.' He was buried at Affane, Co. Waterford.

Concerning Greatrakes, Glanvil states 'the great discourse now at the coffee houses is about Mr. G., the famous Irish stroker. He undergoes various censures here (in London); some take him to be a conjurer, and some an imposter; but others again adore him as an apostle.

'I was three weeks together with him at my Lord Conways', and saw him (I think) lay his hands upon a thousand persons; and really there is something in it more than ordinary; but I am convinced 'tis not miraculous. I have seen pains strangely fly before his hand, till he had chased them out of the body; dimness cleared, and deafness cured by his touch: 20 persons at several times in fits of the falling-sickness (epilepsy) were, in two or three minutes, brought to themselves, so as to tell where their pain was; and when he had pursued it, till he had driven it out at some extreme part; running sores of the King's Evil dried up, and kernels brought to a suppuration by his hand; grievous sores of many months date, in a few days healed; obstructions and stoppings removed, cancerous knots in the breast dissolved etc.

John Pyne, Mary Longdon's employer served as bailiff of Youghal along with Edward P. Percy in 1664. The latter became mayor of Youghal in 1674.

THE WATER EXPERIMENT

The water experiment was carried out as follows: the right thumb was tied to the left great toe and vice-versa. The subject was then thrown into the water and if she sank (and possibly drowned) was declared innocent, but if she floated was said to be a witch. As women's clothing in those days was rather cumbersome, it was inevitable that the woman would float! Water being used in the sacrament of baptism was said to refuse to receive a witch.

IN CO. LOUTH

The Rolls of the Record Office for 1606 of an inquiry at the King's Court in Co. Louth in which one John Aston, late of Mellifont, a clerk, 'not having the fear of God before his eyes, but being wholly seduced by the devil' in the previous December at Mellifont, 'and on divers other days and places, wickedly and feloniously used, practised and exercised divers invocations and conjurings of wicked and lying spirits.'

It was stated he had done so to recover a stolen silver cup, to obtain certain treasures of gold concealed in the earth at Mellifont and Cashel, and to ascertain where Hugh, Earl of Tyrone was abiding. The prisoner, by warrant of the King was sent into England, but nothing further has been traced concerning him.

HOLY CROSS ABBEY

For three and a half centuries until the suppression of the monasteries Holy Cross Abbey, three miles from Thurles was famous for its shrine which was said to contain a relic of the True Cross. It is recorded that in 1609 a pilgrim from Callan (Co. Kilkenny), Anastasia Sobechan 'tortured by magical spells (veneficis incantationibus collisa) at the Abbey in the presence of the Lord Abbot, Brenard (Foulow) placed a girdle around her body that had touched the holy relic.

Suddenly she vomited small pieces of cloth and wood, and for a whole month she spat out from her body such things. She told of this miracle to the Abbot, while she was healed by virtue of the Holy Cross. This he took care to set down in writing.

IN CO. ANTRIM

In 1698 a young Antrim girl innocently put a leaf of sorrel which she had got from a witch into her mouth after she had given the begging witch bread and beer at the door; later she was seized with convulsions and swooned away as if dead. The doctor's remedies proved useless and paroxysms continued.

The minister was sent for: 'scarce had he laid his hand upon her when she was turned by the demon into the most dreadful shapes. She began first to roll herself about, then to vomit needles, pins hairs, feathers, bottoms of thread, pieces of glass, window-nails, nails drawn out of a cart or coach wheel, an iron knife about a span long, eggs and fish shells, and when the witch came near the place, or looked towards the house, even although at a distance of about

200 yards from where the child was, she was in worse torment, insomuch that no life was expected from the child till the witch was removed to some greater distance.'

The witch was apprehended, condemned and refused to recant. She was then strangled and burned.

NOTES

The description of Florence Newton's trial above is taken from notes made by the presiding judge (Sir William Aston) and reproduced in Glanvill's *Sadducismus Triumphatus* (1689). It is unique as an on-the-spot account of a 17th. century witch trial in Ireland. Strangely enough, the judge did not record the verdict, but it is almost certain that Florence suffered the fate of all witches at the time, death by strangulation of fire or both.

CHAPTER 4

ISLAND MAGEE AND THE HELL FIRE CLUB (THE 18 TH CENTURY)

Written down at the time of the event the story of the Island Magee case was printed as a pamphlet in Belfast in 1822, edited by M'Skimin, the author of the History of Carrickfergus. It was entitled: 'A narrative of the sufferings of a young girl called Mary Dunbar, who was strangely molested by spirits and witches at Mr. James Haltridge's house, parish of Island Magee, near Carrickfergus, in the county of Antrim, and province of Ulster, in Ireland, and in some other places to which she was removed during her disorder; as also of the aforesaid Mr. Haltridge's house being haunted by spirits in the latter end of 1710 and beginning of 1711.'

In September 1710 Mrs. Anne Haltridge, widow of Mr. John Haltridge, Presbyterian Minister in Island Magee was sitting at her kitchen fire when small stones were thrown at her, but no-one was in the room at the time. When she retired to bed the curtains of the four-poster were drawn and pulled, and she felt the feet of someone moving over the bed. A few nights later pillows were pulled from under her head and the covering blanket pulled off the bed.

She took a little girl in with her, but the disturbances continued, and although the room was searched nothing could be found to account for the goings on. For a time things became quiet, but one night in December a little boy who appeared to be about 10 or 12 came in and sat down beside her at the fire. He never spoke although questioned, ran in and out, but when it was reported that 'the Master' was coming (Mrs. Haltridge's son, James) he vanished.

On February 11, 1711 Mrs. Haltridge was reading a book. She put it down for a moment, but on looking for it again found it had disappeared. On the next day the strange boy returned, broke a pane of glass in one of the windows and put his hand through and was seen to be holding the missing volume. A servant asked him could he read it and he said he could and that the devil had taught him. He then produced a sword and threatened to kill everyone in the house. The servant ran into the parlour and locked the door.

The boy or 'apparition' laughed and said he could get in through any hole or corner like a cat or a mouse as the devil could make him do anything he pleased. He then took up a large stone, and hurled it through the parlour window. A little after the servant and child looked out, and saw the 'apparition' catching the turkey-cock, which he threw over his shoulder, holding him by the tail; and the bird kicking his feet, the stolen book was knocked out of the loop in the blanket where the boy had put it. He then leaped over a wall with the turkey-cock on his back.

The girl saw him trying to draw his sword to kill the bird, but it escaped. Missing the book out of his blanket he ran nimbly up and down in search of it, and then came with a club and broke the glass of the parlour window. The girl again peeped out and saw him digging with the sword. She summoned up courage to ask him what he was doing, and he answered, 'Making a grave for a corpse which will come out of this house very soon.' He refused, however, to say who it would be and 'flew over the hedge as if he had been a bird.'

SHAPE OF CORPSE

For a day or two following nothing happened, but on the morning of the 15th the clothes were mysteriously taken off Mrs. Haltridge's bed, and laid in a bundle behind it. Being put back by some of the family they were again removed, and this time folded up and placed under a large table which happened to be in the room. Again they were laid in order on the bed, and again they were taken off, and this third time made up in the shape of a corpse, or something that very closely resembled it.

When this strange news spread through the neighbourhood many people came to the house, and, after a thorough investigation, were obliged to acknowledge that there was some invisible agent at work. Mr. Robert Sinclair, the Presbyterian Minister with John Man and Reynold Leaths, two of his Elders, stayed the whole of that day and the following night with the distressed family, spending much of the time in prayer. At night Mrs. Haltridge went to bed as usual in the haunted room, but got very little rest, and at about 12 o'clock she cried out suddenly as if in great pain. When Mr. Sinclair asked what was the matter, she said she felt as if a knife had been stuck into her back.

Next morning she quitted the haunted room and went to another, but the violent pain never left her back, and at the end of the week, on February 22, she died. During her illness the clothes were frequently taken off the bed which she occupied, and made up like a corpse, and even when a table and chairs were laid upon them to keep them on, they were mysteriously removed without any noise, and made up as before; but this never happened when anyone was in the room. The evening before she died they were taken off as usual; but this time, instead of being made up in the customary way, they were folded with great care, and laid in a chest upstairs, where they were only found after a great deal of searching.

We now reach the account of the witch-craft proper, and the consequent trial. About the end of February 1711, Mary Dunbar, aged about 18, whom Dr. Tisdall describes as 'having an open and innocent countenance, and being a very intelligent young person,' came to stay with Mrs. Haltridge, junior, to keep her company after her mother-in-law's death. A rumour was going round that the latter had been bewitched into her grave, and this could not fail to have its effect on Miss Dunbar.

On the night of her arrival her troubles began. When she retired to her bedroom, accompanied by another girl, they were surprised to find that a new mantle and some wearing apparel had been taken out of a trunk and scattered through the house. On looking for the missing articles, they found an apron lying on the parlour floor which two days before had been locked up in another apartment. This apron, when they found it, was rolled up tight, and tied fast with a string of its own material, which had upon it five strange knots.

Having to unloose the knots, she found a flannel cap, which had belonged to old Mrs. Haltridge, wrapped up in a middle of the apron. When she saw this she was frightened, and threw the cap and apron to young Mrs. Haltridge, who also was alarmed, thinking the mysterious knots boded evil to some inmate of the house. That evening Miss Dunbar was seized with a most violent fit, and recovering, cried out that a knife was run through her thigh, and that it was all due to three women, whose appearance she described, but did not then give their names.

About midnight she was seized with a second fit; when she saw in her vision seven or eight women talking together, who called each other by their names. When she came out of her fit she gave their names as Janet Liston, Elizabeth Cellor, Kate M'Calmont, Janet Carson, Janet Mean, Latimer, and one whom they termed Mrs. Ann. She gave so perfect a description of them that several of them were recognised and brought to the 'afflicted,' girl and she picked them out from many other women who were there.

It was reported that as these women were approaching the house Mary Dunbar's fits got worse, and her worst condition was when Latimer was approaching. On recovering the first words she said were, 'O Latimer, Latimer,' and her description agreed exactly to the person. At one time she singled out one of her 'tormentors' among thirty whom they brought in to see if they could deceive her either in the name or description of the accused person. All this was sworn to by persons that were present.

WOMEN ARRESTED

Between March 3 and 24 depositions relative to various aspects of the case were sworn to by several people, and the Mayor of Carrickfergus issued a warrant for the arrest of all suspected persons. Seven women were arrested; their names were:

Janet Mean, of Braid Island.
Jane Latimer, of Irish Quarter, Carrickfergus
Margaret Mitchell, of Kilroot.
Catherine M'Calmont,
Janet Liston, alias Sellar,
Elizabeth Sellar, and
Janet Carson, all of Island Magee.

Her worst 'tormentors' seem to have been taken into custody at an early stage in the proceedings, for Miss Dunbar stated in her deposition, made on March 12 that since their arrest she received no annoyance, except from Mrs. Ann, and another woman blind of an eye, who told her when Mr. Robb the curate, was going to pray with and for her, that she should be little the better for his prayers, for they would hinder her from hearing them, which they accordingly did.'

In one of her attacks Miss Dunbar was informed by this 'Mrs. Ann' that she should never be discovered, by her name, as the rest had been, but she seems to have overlooked the fact that her victim was quite capable of giving an accurate description of her, which she accordingly did, and so was the means of bringing about the apprehension of one Margaret Mitchell, upon which she almost became free from all annoyance.

With regard to the woman blind in one eye we learn from one deponent that three women thus disfigured were brought to her, but she declared they never troubled her.

In one of the earliest of the depositions, that sworn by James Hill on March 5, there is an extraordinary incident recorded, which seems to show that at least one of the accused was a victim of religious mania. He states that on 1st. March 'being in the house of William Sellar of Island Magee, one Mary Tewmain came here and called out Janet Liston to speak to her. When Janet came in again she was trembling, and said the woman asked her to go to Mr. Haltridge's to see Mary Dunbar, but she said she would not go 'for all Island Magee, except Mr. Sinclair would come for her,' and added – 'If the plague of God was on her (Mary Dunbar), the plague of God be on them altogether; the Devil be with them if he was among them. If God had taken her health from her, God give her health: if the Devil had taken it from her, the Devil give it her.'

THE TRIAL BEGINS

The accused were brought up for trial at Carrickfergus before Judges Upton and Macartney on March 31, 1711. Among the witnesses examined were Mr. Skeffington, curate of Larne; Mr. Ogilvie, Presbyterian minister of Larne; Mr. Adair, Presbyterian minister of Carrickfergus; Mr. Cobham, Presbyterian minister of Broad Island; Mr. Edmonstone, of Red Hall, and others. The proceedings at 6 a.m., and lasted until 2 p.m. Many of the witnesses swore that in some of her fits three strong men were scarce able to hold the girl down. She muttered to herself, and spoke some words distinctly, 'told everything she had said in her conversation with the witches, and how she came to say the things, which she spoke when in her fits.'

In her fits she often had her tongue thrust into her windpipe in such a manner that she was like to choke, and the root seemed pulled up into her mouth. Upon her recovery she complained extremely of one Mean, who had twisted her tongue; and told the Court that she had torn her throat, and tortured her violently.

When the woman was called to answer this charge and ordered to show her hand; all the joints were distorted and the tendons shrivelled up, as the girl had described.

One of the men who had held her in a fit swore she had nothing visible on her arms when he took hold of them, and that all in the room saw some worsted yarn tied round her wrist, which was put on invisibly; there were upon this string seven double knots and one single one. In another fit she cried out that she was tormented with a pain about her knee; upon which the women in the room looked at her knee, and found a fillet tied fast about it. Her mother swore it was the one she had given her that morning, and had seen it about her head; this had also seven double knots and one single one.

Her mother was advised by a Catholic priest to use a counter-charm, which was to write some words out of the first chapter of St. John's Gospel in a paper, and to tie the paper with a tape three times round her neck, knotted each time. This the girl declined; but the mother, used it during one of the girls fits. She was being held down by a man, and, recovering a little, complained of a severe pain in her back and about her middle; immediately the company discovered the tape tied round her middle; with seven double knots and one single one. This was sworn to by several witnesses. The man who held the girl was asked by the Judge if it were possible she could reach the tape about her neck while he held her. He said it was not, as he was holding her hand at the time.

During one of her fits, she was observed by several persons to slide off the bed in an unaccountable manner, and to be laid gently on the ground as if supported and drawn invisibly. Upon her recovery she said several persons had drawn her in that manner, with the intention, as they told her, of bearing her out of the window; that she called upon God in her mind and they let her drop on the floor.

Recovering from a fit, she told those present that her tormentors had declared that she should not have power to go over the threshold of the chamberdoor. The evidence declared that they had several times attempted to lead her out of the door, and that she was as often thrown into fits as they had brought her to the said threshold; that to pursue the experiment further they had the threshold taken up, upon which they were immediately struck with so strong a smell of brimstone that they were scarce able to bear it; the stench spread through the whole house, and afflicted several to that degree that they fell sick in their stomachs, and were much disordered.'

There was a great quantity of things produced in Court, and sworn to be what she vomited out of her throat. They included feathers, cotton, yarn, pins, and two large waistcoat buttons.

Her tormentors had told Miss Dunbar that she should have no power to give evidence against them in Court. 'She was accordingly that day before the trial struck dumb, and so continued in Court during the whole trial, but had no violent fit.' said one of those present. 'I saw her in Court cast her eyes about in a wild distracted manner, and it was then thought she was recovering from her fit (of dumbness), and it was hoped she would give her own evidence. I observed, as they were raising her up, she sank into the arms of a person who held her, closed her eyes, and seemed perfectly senseless and motionless. I went to see her after the trial; she told me she knew not where she was when in Court; that she had been afflicted all that time by three persons, of whom she gave a particular description both of their proportion, habits, features, and complexion, and said she had never seen them till the day before the trial.'

The prisoners had no lawyer to defend them, while it is hardly necessary to say that no medical evidence as to the state of health of Miss Dunbar was heard. When the witnesses had been examined the accused were ordered to make their defence. They all positively denied the charge of witchcraft; one with the worst looks, who was therefore the greatest suspect, called God to witness that she was wronged. Their characters were inquired into, and some were reported unfavourable, which seemed to be rather due to their ill appearance than to any facts proved against them. They were nearly all churchgoers.

Judge Upton, summing up said he was of opinion that the jury could not bring them in guilty upon the sole testimony of the afflicted person's visionary images. He said he could not doubt but that the whole matter was preternatural and diabolical, but he conceived that, had the persons accused been really witches and in compact with the Devil, it could hardly be presumed that they should be such constant attenders upon Divine Service, both in public and private.

Unfortunately his Brother on the Bench was not so open-minded. Judge Macartney, differed altogether from him, and thought that the jury might well bring them in guilty. The 12 good men and true lost no time in doing so, and, in accordance with the Statute, the prisoners were sentenced to a year's imprisonment, and to stand in the pillory four times during that period. It is said that when placed in this relic of barbarism the unfortunate wretches were pelted by the mob with eggs and cabbage-stalks to such an extent that one of them had an eye knocked out. And thus ended the last trial for witchcraft in Ireland.

THE HELL FIRE CLUB

A royal edict was issued in England in 1721 condemning 'certain scandalous clubs or societies of young persons who meet together, and in the most impious and blasphemous manner, insult the most sacred principles of our holy religion, affront Almighty

God himself, and corrupt the minds and morals of one another.'

This referred to the notorious Hell Fire Clubs which were then flourishing in many parts of the country. These clubs were indulged in by the more vicious members of the idle rich class. One of the worst of them was that run by Sir Francis Dashwood at Medenham and entitled the 'Medenham Franciscans'. They met in a ruined Cistercian monastery where they indulged in drunken orgies in which women attired as nuns took part.

Dashwood was also the first 'Superior' of the Hell Fire Club in England. In both organisations religion was mocked, there were parodies of the Mass and other blasphemous activities. The 'committee' of the club was composed of twelve members, with a 'Devil' in charge in mockery of the Last Supper.

In a pamphlet published in 1721 it was stated men and women members adopted the dress of religious orders, assumed the names of saints, martyrs and prophets, whom they caricatured in their mock religious ceremonies.

On the top of Montpelier Hill near Rathfarnham stands the ruins of Dublin's Hell Fire Club – a landmark to dwellers in the capital for nearly 250 years. It was said to be frequented by members of the Dublin branch of that infamous society. Wild carousings and sacrilegious ceremonies were said to have been carried out there, and up to the present day few people will go near the ruins after dark.

The Irish Hell Fire Club was organised by Richard Parsons, first Earl of Rosse and Colonel Jack St. Leger, and confined its membership to men, the majority being recruited from the leading 'bucks' of the period. St. Leger lived in a magnificent country mansion, 'Grangemellon' near Athy where he entertained lavishly, and many stories were told about the wild orgies held there.

A regular meeting place of the club in Dublin was the Eagle Tavern on Cork Hill which was the setting for James Worsdale's famous painting which is in the National Gallery in Dublin. Painted about 1735 it shows a group of five men seated around a table on which reposes a huge punch-bowl.

The group consists of Henry Barry, fourth Lord Santry, Colonel Clements, Colonel Ponsonby, Colonel St. George and Simon Luttrell of Luttrellstown, afterwards first Earl of Carhampton. The punch-bowl contained the club's special beverage-scaltheen (whiskey and butter). A black cat, supposed to represent the devil presided, and sometimes when the meetings ended after midnight a member of the club emerged as Satan, wearing the skin, tail and horns of a cow, to the terror of any citizens who happened to be around at the time.

On one occasion the large tom cat was immersed in the scaltheen and set on fire. It was pushed outside the door, and when it appeared, the crowd who had gathered to the ribald shouts and singing inside, seeing a fierce screaming animal with flames leaping from it, rushing straight at them, they thought the devil had really appeared and fled for their lives.

The club's activities began about 1720, and lasted until about 1740 when most of the members had either died or gone to England. There were two other similar clubs in Ireland at the time – the Blasters, founded by the miniaturist, Peter Lens and the Limerick Hell Fire Club which had one female member, a Mrs Blennerhasset.

It was probably during the summer months that the group met in Montpelier House, which was originally built as a shooting lodge by the Right Honourable William Connolly of Castletown, Speaker of the Irish House of Commons, about the year 1725, shortly after he purchased the Duke of Wharton's estate in the neighbourhood. Up to that time a large cairn, or cromlech had stood on the spot, and the stones from this pre-historic monument were used to build part of the house.

Not so long after the house was completed the slated roof was blown off one night in a tremendous storm. Local people said this was caused by the agency of the devil in retaliation for desecrating the old cairn. The orgies on Montpelier continued even after the abolition of the English Hell Fire Clubs, but suddenly ended after the death of a servant under inhuman conditions which resulted in a public outcry.

After a drunken revel the unfortunate man's clothes had been soaked by the members in whiskey and set alight, and he died as a result. It was only poetic justice when shortly afterwards the building itself was burned down, leaving the stone shell as a reminder of evil days that have passed.

NOTE

James Macartney became second puisne Justice of the King's Bench in 1701, puisne Justice of Common Pleas in 1714, and retired in 1726. Anthony Upton became puisne Justice of Common Pleas, was succeeded as above, and committed suicide in 1718. Both were natives of Co. Antrim.

CHAPTER 5

CARRICKFERGUS (THE 19TH CENTURY)

THE BALLAD OF MARY BUTTERS

An unusual trial took place at the Spring Assizes in Carrickfergus in March, 1808. The events which led to it were reported in the Belfast Newsletter of August 21, 1807 and recorded by M'Skimin in his *Historical Notices of Old Belfast*.

A tailor named Alexander Montgomery lived in a house near Carrickfergus Meeting House. He had a cow which was yielding plenty of milk, but for some unknown reason no butter could be made with the milk. His wife, having listened to some old women's talk locally said that the cow must be bewitched.

She was told that a wise woman, Mary Butters of Carnmoney would rid them of the spell that was on the animal, so the husband went off and fetched her. The old woman was brought to the house (one night in August, 1807), and at about 10 o'clock set about working her spells.

First of all she ordered the tailor and a young man named Carnaghan to go into the cow-house, turn their waistcoats inside out and stand by the head of the cow until she sent for them, while the tailor's wife, son and an old woman named Margaret Lee stayed in the house with her.

The men kept a lonely vigil until daybreak, when getting no summons, they left their post and knocked at the door of the house. There was no answer. They then looked through the kitchen window, and to their

> In Carrick town a wife did dwell
> Who does pretend to conjure witches,
> Auld Barbara Goats, or Lucy Bell,
> Ye'll no lang to come through her clutches.
> A woeful trick this wife did play
> On simple Sawney, our poor tailor.
> She mittimissed the other day
> To lie in Limbo with the jailor

horror saw the inmates stretched on the floor as if dead. They burst in the door and found that the tailor's wife and son were indeed dead, and Mary Butters and Margaret Lee nearly so. While they were there the latter expired, but on kicking Mary Butters she revived.

The house had a sulphurous smell, and on the fire was a large pot containing among other ingredients, milk, needles, pins, and crooked nails. All the windows and doors of the house had been stuffed.

At an inquest held later the jury brought in a verdict that the four victims had died of suffocation caused by Mary Butters' noxious ingredients, prepared after the manner of a charm to bring about the cure of the sick cow. The Assizes discharged Mary Butters by proclamation. Her version was that a black man had appeared with a huge club, killed three and stunned herself.

A racy ballad was composed about the occurrence by a resident, which is unique as it is possibly the only ballad about an Irish witch extant. It was quoted in the Ulster Journal of Archaeology for 1908. Here it is:

This simple Sawney had a cow,
Was aye as sleekit as an other;
It happened for a month or two
Aye when they churned they got no butter.
Rown-tree tied in the cow's tail,
And vervain glean'd about the ditches;
These breets and charms did not prevail,
They could not banish the auld witches.

The neighbour wives a' gathered in
In number near about a dozen;
Elspie Dough and Mary Linn,
An' Kate M'Cart, the tailor's cousin.
Aye they churned and aye they swat,
Their aprons loos'd, and loost their mutches;
But yet nae butter they could get,
They blessed the cow but curst the witches.

Had Sawney summoned all his wits
And sent away for Huie Mertin,
He could have gall'd the witches' guts,
An' cured the kye for Nannie Barton.
But he may show the farmer's wab,
An' long wade through the money gutters;
Alas! it was a sore mis-job
When he employ'd auld Mary Butters.

The sorceress opens the scene
With magic words of her invention,
To make the foolish people keen
Who did not know her base intention
She drew a circle round the churn,
And washed the staff in south-run water,
And swore the witches she would burn,
But she would have the tailor's butter.

When sable night her curtain spread
Then she got on a flaming fire;
The tailor stood at the cow's head
With his turn'd waistcoat in the byre.
The chimney covered with a scraw
An' every crevice where it smoak'd,
But long before the cock did craw
The people in the house were choak'd.

The muckle pot hung on all night,
As Mary Butters had been brewing
In hopes to fetch some witch or wight,
Whas entrails by her art were stewing.
In this her magic a' did fail,
Nae witch nor wizard was detected,
Now Mary Butters lies in jail
For the base part that she has acted.

The tailor lost his son and wife,
For Mary Butters did them smother;
But as he hates a single life
In four weeks time he got another.
He is a crouse, aul canty chiel,
An' care nae what the witches mutter;
He'll never mair employ the Deil,
Nor his auld agent Mary Butters.

At day the tailor left his post
Though he had seen no apparition,
Nae wizard grim, nae witch nor ghost,
Though still he had a stray suspicion
That some auld wizard wrinkled wife
Had cast her cantrips o'er poor Brawney
Cause she and he did live in strife,
An' wha's the man can blame poor Sawney.

Wae sucks for our young lasses now,
For who can read their mystic matters,
Or tell if their sweethearts be true,
The folks a' run to Mary Butters
To tell what thief a horse did steal,
In this she was a mere pretender
An' has nae art to raise the Deil
Like that auld wife the Witch of Endor.

If Mary Butters be a witch
Why but the people all should know it,
An' if she can the Muses touch
I'm sure she'll soon descry the poet.
Her ain familiar off she'll sen'
Or paughlet wi a tu' commission
To pour her vengeance on the man
That tantalizes her condition.

CHAPTER 6

THE CLONMEL BURNING (THE 19TH CENTURY)

And he saw young men and young girls
Who danced on a level place,
And Bridget his bride among them,
With a sad and a gay face.
    'The Host of the Air' (W. B. Yeats)

In his *Irish Fairy and Folk Tales* W. B. Yeats writes as follows – 'Sometimes the fairies fancy mortals, and carry them away into their own country, leaving instead some sickly fairy child, or a log of wood so bewitched that it seems to be a mortal pining away, and dying, and being buried... If you overlook a child, that is look at it with envy, the fairies have it in their power. Many things can be done to find out is a child a changeling, but there is one infallible thing-lay it on the fire with this formula, "Burn, burn, burn-if of the devil, burn; but if of God and the saints, be safe from harm" (given by Lady Wilde). Then if it be a changeling it will rush up the chimney with a cry, for according to Giraldus Cambrensis, "fire is the greatest of enemies to every kind of phantom, in so much that those who have seen apparitions fall into a swoon as soon as they are sensible of the brightness of fire.' "

Yeats says that Lady Wilde also gives the gloomy tradition that there are two kinds of fairies-one kind, merry and gentle, the other evil, and sacrificing every year a life to Satan, for which purpose they steal mortals. In his play *Ill Met by Moonlight*, Micheal Mac-Liammoir gives us a changeling in a modern Connemara setting. It is not so long ago that this folk tradition resulted in a grim tragedy in rural Ireland.

In March, 1894 rumours were afloat in the neighbourhood concerning the mysterious disappearance of Bridget Cleary, aged about 26, the wife of Michael Cleary of Ballyvadlea, a lonely district a short distance from Cloneen, between that village and Mullinahone in Co. Tipperary.

A short time later, Michael Cleary, Patrick Boland (father of Bridget Cleary), John Dunne, Patrick, James, Michael and Mary Kennedy, and William Ahearne were brought before the Magistrates, charged with assaulting and ill-treating Bridget Cleary on March 14, and causing her actual bodily harm. Her body had not then been found.

The prisoners were remanded, and search was made for the missing woman. On Friday, March 22, the body was discovered, buried in a cramped position, in a piece of swampy land, about a quarter of a mile from Cleary's house. An inquest was held, and the jury returned a verdict of death caused by extensive burns. These burns, as the evidence showed, were on the abdomen, the lower part of the back and the left hand.

On the resumption of the magisterial inquiry, in addition to the prisoners already named, William Kennedy and Denis Ganey, a herb-doctor, were also included in the charges.

All the Kennedys were cousins of the dead woman, except Mary Kennedy, who was her aunt. The report of the proceedings appeared in the 'Irish Times' of March 26, 27 and 28, and April 2, 3, 6 and 8.

The most important witness for the Crown was Mrs Johannah Burke, wife of a labourer living at Rath Kenney near the Clearys. She stated that on the night of Thursday, March 14 she went up to see

Mrs Cleary who was sick and met William Simpson and his wife outside the door of the house, which was locked. Witness asked for admittance, but Michael Cleary said they would not open the door. While they remained outside they stood at the window.

They heard someone inside saying: 'Take it you witch.' When the door was opened witness went in and saw Dunne and three of the Kennedys holding Mrs Cleary down on her bed by her hands and feet, and her husband was giving her milk and herbs in a spoon out of a saucepan.

They forced her to take the herbs, said Mrs Burke, and Cleary asked: 'Are you Bridget Boland, the wife of Michael Cleary, in the name of God?' She answered it once or twice, and her father asked a similar question. Michael Cleary (the witness thought) then threw a certain liquid on his wife. They put the question to her again, and she repeated the words after them. John Dunne then said: 'Hold her on the fire and she will soon answer.'

Cleary and Patrick Kennedy then lifted Mrs Cleary off the bed, and placed her in a kind of sitting position over the kitchen fire, which was a slow one. Mrs Cleary's appearance had greatly changed. She seemed to be wild and deranged, especially while they were so treating her. While they held her near the fire she was only wearing her nightdress and chemise. They repeated the question and she answered: 'I am Bridget Boland, daughter of Patrick Boland in the name of God.' The witness said she screamed and cried out to her: 'Oh, Han, Han!'

They put her back to bed about 11 o'clock. They all stayed in the house until 6 o'clock next morning, except Dunne and Ahearne, who went after 2 o'clock. Mrs Cleary never went to sleep. She was nervous and not sensible. At one time she said: 'the police are at the window; let you mind me now.'

The following evening the witness went with her daughter Katty to Cleary's house, and found Cleary in bed. The witness prepared some milk for her. Later on Mrs Cleary asked if the witness was paid for the milk, and she answered 'yes', and showed her the shilling which she took and put under the blankets, but gave it back again in a minute. Subsequently when Mrs Cleary was sitting at the fire with her husband, he said she had rubbed the shilling to her leg. She got angry at that, and said she did not rub it to her leg — that there were no 'pishogues' about her.

Other persons came into the house, among them several of the accused, and Bridget Cleary was dressed and brought down into the kitchen. 'Her father, my brother and myself, and deceased and her husband sat at the fire. They were talking about the fairies, and Mrs Cleary said to her husband, 'Your mother used to go with the fairies, and that is why you think I am going with them. He asked her: 'Did my mother tell you that?' She said: 'She did; that she gave two nights with them.'

'I made tea and offered Bridget Cleary a cup of it. Her husband got three bits of bread and jam and said she should eat them before she should take a sup. He asked her: "Are you Bridget Cleary, my wife, in the name of God?" She answered twice and ate two pieces of bread and jam. When she did not answer the third time, he forced her to eat the third bit, saying, "if you won't take it, down you will go." '

'He flung her on the ground, put his knee on her chest, one hand on her throat, and forced the bit of bread and jam down her throat saying: "Swallow it. Is it down? Is it down?" . . . I said, "Mike let her alone, don't you see it is Bridget that is in it?", meaning that it was Bridget his wife and not the fairy, for he suspected that it was a fairy, and not his wife that was there.'

'Michael Cleary then stripped his wife's clothes off, except her chemise, and got a lighting stick out of the fire. She was lying on the floor, and he held it near her mouth. My mother and brothers and myself wanted to leave the house when he flung her on the floor, but Michael Cleary had the key of the door in his pocket, and said the door was not to be opened until he got his wife back.'

District-Inspector Wansborough, prosecuting asked: 'Did you see him throw the lamp oil on her?' – 'I did.'

'Did she say anything when she was burning?' – 'She did. She turned and called out to me, in a mournful tone, "Oh, Han, Han." '

'What did you reply?' – 'I endeavoured to get out for the peelers. My brother, when he could not get the key, went up into the other room and fell into a weakness. My mother threw Easter water on him.'

Where was Bridget Cleary all this time?' – 'She was burning on the hearth. The house was full of smoke and smell. I had to go up to the room. I could not stand. When I looked down to the kitchen I saw the remains of Bridget Cleary on the floor, lying on a sheet. She was lying on her face, and her legs turned upwards, as if they had contracted in the burning.'

The unfortunate woman was then dead. The witness then said that Michael Cleary came up into the room where she was and took out a large sack. He said: 'hold your tongue, Hannah. It is not Bridget I am burning. You will soon see her (meaning the changeling) go up in the chimney.'

He went down to the kitchen with the sack, and when I looked down again the body had been burned. When she was burning, Michael Cleary screamed out – 'she is burning now, but God knows I did not mean to do it. I may thank Jack Dunne for all of it.' Cleary and witness's brother, Patrick then took the body away to bury it.

Some additional particulars were given by other witnesses who were called to corroborate this horrible story. Katie Burke, a little girl, daughter of Johannah Burke said that Michael Cleary knocked his wife down when she would not eat the third bit of bread. 'Then he got a red stump and told her he would put it down her mouth if she would not eat a bit. She again refused, and he caught her and laid her on the fire. He got lamp oil and put it on her, and she blazed up. When she was burning John Dunne and William Kennedy roared for the key, but they did not get it.

'William Kennedy and Mrs Burke tried to get the key ... then they went into the room and witness heard Michael Cleary say: "Go up the chimey!" but did not know what name he called her. Mrs Cleary was burning, and witness saw a sheet on the floor.'

William Simpson of Ballyvadlea, caretaker, who it will be remembered, met Mrs Burke outside the door of Cleary's cottage on the Thursday evening was next examined, said when he went inside he heard loud shouts of 'Away she go!, away she go!' He could not say whose voice it was, but he thought the men who were holding the deceased were saying it. John Dunne was holding her by the head; Pat Kennedy was holding her arm on the right side; James was holding on the left side; William Kennedy was holding her by the legs ... deceased was lying upon her back ... she appeared to be in pain. She shouted and screamed a little at that time. She screamed more afterwards than she did then.

Mrs Cleary's husband was standing by the bed. He was holding a saucepan in both hands. He asked his wife – 'Are you Bridget Boland, the wife of Michael

Cleary, in the name of the Father, Son and Holy Ghost?' She said some reply to the effect – 'Yes, I am.' The questions were repeated several times; she only answered a few times.

Witness saw Michael Cleary afterwards giving his wife some liquids in a spoon out of the saucepan. Asked what was in the saucepan witness said: 'I don't know, but I heard that it was herbs. I did not hear that anything else was put in it. I heard Michael Cleary say he got some herbs from Ganey .. Cleary was pouring the herbs into the mouth of the deceased. She resisted by keeping her mouth closed. The liquid was forced in. Besides this water was poured over her by direction of Michael Cleary, and this lasted for 10 or 20 minutes. The father and husband were asking her questions in the meantime.

They apparently repeated again and again the question already mentioned. There were now 13 persons in the room, including the witness. Colonel Evanson, the presiding Magistrate asked: 'In your opinion, what were they there for?' – 'To hunt away the witches and the fairies. The door was open for that purpose. I don't know that they came for that purpose, but when they were there, they were at that work. I went to see Mrs Cleary.'

The witness was asked: 'Did Mrs Cleary reply at all to the questions put to her?' – 'She did when she was on the fire. Her brother asked her: "Are you the daughter of Patrick Boland, the wife of Michael Cleary. Answer in the name of God!" She answered, "I am dada." Her husband asked her a similar question, and she said, "Yes, I am." Those questions were answered repeatedly by her. They were then satisfied that they had their own.'

'What do you mean by that?' – 'That they had Mrs Cleary and not a witch.'

'Then what had they got before?' – 'They believed that they had a witch. About 20 minutes before she was taken off the bed she screamed terribly. That was when the mixture went down. They also shook her then and slapped her hands. The same men held her from start to finish. When they were shaking her they all said: "Away with you! Come home, Bridget Boland in the name of God." '

After deceased was removed from the fire and fresh clothes put on her 'she was then asked by her husband did she know the persons standing around her and she said "yes". He showed her one of the Kennedys in particular and asked her what relation he was to her, and she said her first cousin, and he asked her in turn did she know each person in the room and she said she did. They were all satisfied then that they had her. They were all speaking and saying – "Do you think it is her that is here?" and the answer would be "Yes," and they were all delighted at it." '

All this took place on Thursday, March 14, the first of the two days spoken of by Mrs Burke. Simpson gave further important evidence. He said he saw Michael Cleary on the road on the same day that he heard Mrs Cleary was missing (apparently Sunday, March 16) and again on the following Sunday. Cleary said that his wife left the house on Friday night. Witness believed him. He saw Cleary again about 7 or 8 that evening when he asked witness for the loan of a revolver. He said that those parties who had convinced him about his wife would not go with him to the fort.

Asked what was meant by that the witness said: 'It appeared to me that they had convinced him that his wife had gone to the fort.'

'What was the fort?' – 'The fort at Kylegranagh

Hill. It appeared to me that they had convinced him that his wife had gone with the fairies, and that they had convinced him so far he should see it out with them.'

'He wanted a revolver to force them to go?' – 'Yes. The fort was reported to be a fairies' habitation. Cleary said he expected to meet her at the fort.'

'Did he say how he expected her to appear?' – 'He said she would be riding a grey horse, and she had told him so. And he said that they should cut the ropes that were tying her on the saddle, and she would then stay with him if he was able to keep her.' The witness then said he did not lend Cleary a revolver, but afterwards saw Cleary with a big table knife in his pocket to bring to the fort with him.

Mary Simpson, wife of William Simpson corroborated the statements. She also said that when the door was opened on the Thursday evening, and she and her husband went in with Mrs Burke and her daughter, she heard the men inside there say – 'Away she goes, away she goes!', as though they were driving something out of the house. It appeared to her that they did not believe Mrs Cleary was there, and that they wanted to drive away what was in the bed – 'they thought it was a witch, but I did not.'

She further stated that when Cleary was giving his wife the herbs, he said: 'Take that in the name of God,' and 'Bridget Cleary, come back to me in the name of God!'

Rev. Cornelius F. Ryan said he was curate of the parish of Drangan and the Clearys were members of his congregation and under his spiritual care. He had known them for about a year and a half, and never observed any signs of mental derangement in Mrs Cleary until he attended her almost immediately before her death on March 13.

As far as he could say, she and her husband were living on good terms with one another. When he visited her on the afternoon of the 13th. she was in bed. She appeared to be in a very nervous state, and, as he thought, possibly hysterical. He came to the conclusion that it might be the beginning of mental derangement. She did not converse with him except as a priest; and her conversation was quite coherent and intelligible.

Father Ryan said he administered the last rites of the Church to her on that occasion, and on Friday May 15, he came again, being summoned by Cleary and celebrated Mass in her room.

The witness was asked by the District Inspector: 'Is it possible that you heard nothing of these proceedings about witchcraft?' He replied – 'Up to that time I heard nothing, absolutely nothing.'

'Don't you think that very extraordinary?' enquired the Inspector. 'No,' he replied, 'I do not. The priest is very often the last to hear of things like that – generally, I should say. I heard a rumour on the Saturday after, that Mrs Cleary had disappeared mysteriously. I had no suspicion of foul play or witchcraft, and if I had I would have absolutely refused to say Mass in the house, and have given information to the police at once.'

Dr. Crean gave evidence that he attended Mrs Cleary on March 13, and found her suffering from slight bronchial catarrh and nervous excitement.

When all the evidence was concluded all the prisoners except Ganey (who was discharged) were committed for trial on the charge of wilful murder. Some of them made statements on their committal. Boland, among other things said – 'Cleary said to me. "Have you any faith? Don't you know it is with an old witch I am sleeping?" I said: "You are not. You are sleeping with my daughter." '

Mary Kennedy said that on the Wednesday she was sent for by Michael Cleary to go down and see his wife. She went down and saw her, and she complained of suffering from a pain in her head. She said that Michael Cleary was making a fairy of her, and that he had tried to burn her three months before.

John Dunne said that after the murder Cleary told him – 'She was not my wife, she was too fine to be my wife. She was two inches taller than my wife.' Dunne said that after going to the priest on the sunday, Cleary asked him (Dunne) would he go and help him to look for his wife at the fort that evening. He replied that he would not; that it was all 'moonshine.' Cleary told him that it was a strange woman and not his wife that he burned.

James Kennedy stated that 'They', meaning apparently his brother William, Cleary and himself 'went three nights to the fort at Kylenagranagh, but did not see anything.'

The trial took place at Clonmel on July 4 and 5, 1894 before Mr Justice O'Brien and a jury. Little was added to the evidence already given, but the following is worth mentioning: –

Mrs Burke, cross-examined by Dr. Falconer, said she was in Cleary's house when Cleary said to William Simpson that the house was full of fairies. That was on Thursday. He said that not one fairy was going out of the door, but several.

'At the time the body was burned, was the Rosary said?' – 'Yes. At the time the body was laid on the sheet, my mother said: "In the name of God let you go anywhere and say the Rosary. It was the devil that whispered it into his ears." Cleary then said to Dunne – "I have something here that will make her alright." Dunne said – "It is not today you have a right to get anything for her; it is not in Fethard you had a right to be for a doctor. Three days ago you had a right to be beyond with Ganey, for the doctor had nothing to do with her. It is not your wife is there. You will have enough to do to bring her back. This is the eighth day and you had a right to have gone to Ganey on the fifth day." He added that the herbs should be given to her on the fifth day.'

'Did he mention the name of the herb?' Did he say it was lusmore?' – 'No, he said it was the seventh brother of the seventh sister, or something like that. He said that it was the last herb that could be given to her, and he said it was either kill or cure. He had herbs in his hand, and he gave instructions to Michael Cleary to boil them, and make the Sign of the Cross, and go round the house making pishrogues.'

'Cleary asked Dunne was he doing it right and he said that he was. Then Cleary went round the house making pishrogues and charms. Dunne whispered to Cleary, so that I should not hear what the charm was. Cleary made no fairy of her, it was all Dunne's fault. Cleary was fond of his wife, and had the priest to attend her.'

In the latter statement, as the judge pointed out to the jury, the witness was trying to screen her relative, Cleary, at the expense of Dunne.

The result of the trial was that all defendants were found guilty of manslaughter, and sentenced to various terms of penal servitude and imprisonment, the longest sentence, 20 years penal servitude being imposed on Cleary.

The following rhyme, based on the evidence, and which shows that the name was pronounced in the Gaelic way locally, is still recalled in Co. Tipperary: –

> Are you a witch; are you a fairy?
> Or are you the wife of Michael Cleary?

NOTES

The mention of water thrown over Mrs Cleary – this was probably a concoction of urine and hen's excrement, which was the pishrogue in such cases.

Shaking – To get back a child from the fairies, the 'changeling' was placed sitting on a shovel and swung backwards and forewards to the incantation – 'If you be a fairy, away with you!'

Lusmore (Foxglove) – the cure from this was three drops on the tongue and three in each ear.

Fairy Mistress – In his book, *Witchcraft Today*, the late Gerald B. Gardner writes: 'The Fairy Mistress was a recognised type called the Leannan Sidhe. She was good and beautiful, but dangerous, and you must not beat her or she would run back to her own people, taking her dowry of fairy cattle and her children with her. Usually she exacted a promise not to tell of her fairy origin; therefore she must have been of such a size to be taken for a mortal. Women sometimes had fairy husbands, but they usually had to keep it a secret, or sometimes it was just the fact that he was a fairy that was kept secret, which also tends to show his size. 'In Scotland the fairy mistress often helped her husbands with his craft; she could foretell his future, when he would die, or whom he would marry after her death or after she left him; but while the association lasted she was usually very jealous. Fairy mistresses were said to steal babies and probably they did so to make the race grow stronger. Beautiful girls were regularly kidnapped as brides for the Fairy King, and male fairies often persuaded girls to leave home.'

CHAPTER 7

THE WITCH IN FOLKLORE

The witch or Wise Woman, as she is more popularly called, has an important place in Irish folklore, and probably was originally a Sibyl in Druidic times. She remained an important member of the community up to comparatively recent times, giving cures for cows' diseases and for other animal ailments, and perhaps occasionally arranging matches, and providing the young maidens with love-potions.

Regarding the darker side of her art, here is what W. B. Yeats says in *Irish Fairy and Folk Tales:* –
'The spells of the witch smell of the grave. One of the most powerful is the charm of the dead hand. With a hand cut from a corpse, they, muttering words of power, will stir a well and skim from its surface a neighbour's butter.'

'A candle held between the fingers of the dead hand can never be blown out. This is useful to robbers, but they appeal for the suffrage of the lovers likewise, for they can make love-potions by drying and grinding into powder the liver of a black cat. Mixed with tea, and poured from a black teapot, it is infallible.'

The bewitching of butter and cows were common charges against local witches. Miss Letitia MacLintock tells of a case in Rathmullan, Co. Donegal, where one family was jealous of another's fine Kerry cow. After a girl of the former family had milked the cow in question it stopped giving milk. The advice of a local sage, a man this time, was sought.

He told the woman of the house to lock the door

and get nine new pins that were never used in clothes, and to put them in a saucepan with a pint of milk, put them on the fire and boil them. When the pins began to simmer in the milk steps were heard approaching the door, and an agitated girl's voice cried out – 'Let me in. Take off that cruel pot! Take out the pins, for they're pricking holes in my heart, and I'll never touch that milk of yours again.'

In June, 1890, at Dungannon Quarter Sessions before Sir Francis Brady, one farmer sued another for breach of warranty in a cow. It was stated that the animal had been 'blinked' or bewitched, and the defendant described how a visit had been paid to a Wise Woman, who instructed him in an elaborate curative charm.

In 1892 a man related that a friend of his living in the Aran Islands was stricken with an incurable disease, and having been given up by his doctor, he sought the services of a cailleach, an old woman, able by her occult power to transfer the malady from the sufferer to some healthy person, who would sicken fast and die in consequence.

Her method was to go to a field adjoining the highway, and there to pluck certain herbs from the ground, looking up at the public as she did so. The first passer-by, on whom her malignant glance lighted would in 24 hours take the sick man's illness and quickly die, the other recovering in the same time.

THE WOMAN OF SCARAWALSH

Patrick Kennedy, in his *Legends and Fictions of the Irish Celts* tells of an old woman of Scarawalsh, Co. Wexford, who lived in bad repute with her neighbours. She was seen on Mary Eve skimming a well on a neighbouring farm. She then went into an adjoining meadow and skimmed the dew off the grass. One person said he heard her murmuring – 'come all to me and none to he.'

In a day of two, the owner of the farm, coming in from the fields about noon, found the family still at the churn, and no sign of butter. He looked here and there, and at last spied a piece of stale butter fastened to the mantel beam of the open fireplace.

'That's witches butter,' said one of the girls, 'cut it off.'

'No use' said another, 'only a charmed knife could do that.' The master of the house, having got advice then did as follows – they twisted twigs of the mountain ash around their cows' necks; they made a big fire, and thrust into it the sock and coulter of the plough; they fastened the ash twigs round the churn, and connected them to the chain of the plough-irons; shut door and windows, so that they could not be opened from outside, and merrily began the churning.

When the plough irons were red-hot, someone tried the latch of the door, and next they saw the face of the witch outside the window. 'What do you want?' asked the master. She replied, 'The seed of the fire. I want to keep you at the churning.' Then she roared, for the burning plough irons were scorching her inside.

After further appeals by the witch were unsuccessful, and she had been further tormented by the irons she gave in and said – 'Throw the bit of butter you'll find in this sheet of paper into the churn, and this sod of turf into the fire, and cut away the bit of butter on the mantel beam with this knife, and give it back to me, till I return it to the knowledgeable woman I begged it from for you.'

When these directions were followed, the butter

began to appear in heaps in the churn. There was great rejoicing, and they even wanted to entertain the old rogue. But she departed in rage, saying, 'I won't take bite or sup from you. Ye have treated me like a Hessian, or a Cromwellian, and not like an honest neighbour, so I leave my curse and the curse of Cromwell on ye all!'

THE WITCH HARE

Witches in Ireland were said to be able to change at will into either a hare or a cat. Stories of the witch-hare are common in the West. They were said to be responsible for cows becoming dry by emerging at night as hares and sucking the milk from the cattle. Giraldus Cambrensis recorded this in the 12th century as happening in England Wales and Scotland as well as Ireland.

One of the tales about the witch-hare goes as follows – A hunt is in progress when the dogs suddenly come upon a hare, injuring it before it escapes. After a long chase, the hare eventually dashes through the open doorway of a small cottage. The Master of the Hunt dismounts and goes inside the cottage. An old, old woman is bent over an open fireplace.

The Master asks did a hare go inside, and the old woman, blowing and panting all the time, shakes her head. Then the Master notices that the old woman has an injury corresponding to that of the hare, and recognises her as a witch.

Another story current in folklore is the sinking of ships at sea by the violent moving of water in a vessel, or by boiling the water, this causing a fierce storm at sea. Then by turning the dish upside down, the ship would also turn over and drown the occupants.

PUCK FAIR

The little village of Killorglin in Country Kerry is the scene every year of the famous 'Puck Fair and Pattern' which lasts for three days – August 10th., Gathering Day; August 11th., Puck's Fair Day and August 12th., Scattering Day or Children's Day. On the evening of Gathering Day a procession assembles, and to the accompaniment of great jollifications a large Puck(male) goat, preferably a white one, with his horns bedecked with ribbons and rosettes is borne in triumph in a lorry through the streets to a high platform in the square in the centre of the town.

'King Puck' remains there for the next two days, presiding over the business of the Fair, and being well fed with large succulent cabbages. On the second day all the commercial undertakings – sales of horses, cattle etc. take place. On Scattering Day gaily dressed children begin to dethrone the 'King.' Puck is brought again around the town to the sounds of music and revelry, and over the bridge across the River Laune, back to where he came from, and turned loose to wander once again his native hills. His reign is over for another year.

Apart from the fact that the Fair was originally associated with the Festival of Lughnasa, one of the four great Festivals of Ancient Ireland, little is known as to how it originated. It has been mentioned as far back as the 17th century. A local tradition maintains that the Fair was transferred to Killorglin from Kilgobnet, a small village with a ruined church at the foot of the MacGillicuddy Reeks four miles to the south-east.

It is quite possible that it is a survival of an old pagan rite, but most unlikely that it has anything to do with the horned god of the witches. Perhaps there is a connection with that strange animal, linked with the devil in folklore – the Puca.

Douglas Hyde tells of a horse-like creature who used to frequent a certain hill in Leinster and would appear every November Day and answer questions in a human voice. But that, says Dr. Hyde, was before the coming of Christianity. November Day was said to be sacred to the Puca, and he was said to take many shapes – horse, ass, bull, goat or eagle.

At the Mullinavat Fair in Co. Kilkenny a goat was also enthroned, and at Cappawhite Fair in Co. Tipperary a whitewashed horse was paraded and put on display on top of an earthen fort.

BUYING THE SHEAF

'Buying the Sheaf,' a practice of the black art, was still being carried out in 1893 in Co. Louth. The person first visited a church, with back mockingly turned to the altar as witches do, muttered certain words. A sheaf of wheat was selected and shaped like the human body, the head being made like pleated straw. Into this and at the various joints pins were deeply stuck, and with horrid invocation of the devil the sheaf was buried near the home of the intended victim. As the wheat rotted, the victim sickened, expiring when it was completely decomposed. This was mentioned at a court case in Ardee in 1893.

Douglas Hyde tells of the 'reversed journey.' This involves making the Stations of the Cross backwards in a church, all the time invoking the devil, and asking him to send misfortunes and bad luck on a hated enemy.

POSTSCRIPT

Is witchcraft being carried out in Ireland today? A discovery in Island Magee, Co. Antrim (where Mary Dunbar had her strange experiences as described in Chapter Four) in October, 1961 indicate that it is. A party of cyclists out for a Sunday spin from Belfast were exploring a cave known appropriately enough, as 'The Devil's Hideout' at Island Magee, when one of them lifted a large stone and discovered underneath a number of black cloaks, black candles, the effigy of a serpent's head in wood, a decanter and two glass wine vessels.

They were enclosed in a cardboard box. Police from Belfast and Whitehead, who investigated the articles, said that because of the accumulated dust on some of the articles, and the fact that rats had been nibbling at the cloaks, it was obviously some time since the objects had been used. They said, however, the articles might also have been put there for future use.

One of the documents found included the terms of an oath renouncing everything Christian and good, and pledging support of things evil. There were rumours of a cult calling itself, 'The Brotherhood of the Lefthand Path' which required followers to sign an oath with their own blood. They have their own 'Black Calendar' as opposed to the Calendar of the Saints, and their rituals are designed to blaspheme Christian practices.

The cave is about a mile long and part of it is underground, and it is one of the few caves in the famous Gobbin's cliff face that can be reached by boat.
June 23, 1966

BIBLIOGRAPHY

Barton, Sir Plunket – Links between Ireland and Shakespeare
Cambrensis, Giraldus – Topographica Hibernia
Camden Society – The Trial of Dame Alice Kyteler for Witchcraft (1843)
Folklore, Volume VI, 1895
Gardner, Gerald B. – Witchcraft Today
Glanvil, Joseph – Sadducismus Triumphatus. Or a Full and Plain Evidence concerning Witches and Apparitions (London, 1689)
Kennedy, Patrick – Legends and Fictions of the Irish Celts
MacNeill, Maire – The Feast of Lughnasa
M'Skimin, – The Island Magee Case (Belfast, 1822)
Historical Notices of Old Belfast
O Duilearga, Seamus – Leabhar Sheain I Chonaill
O'Grady, Standish – Silva Gadelica
Rees, Alwyn and Brinley – Celtic Heritage
Rich, Barnaby – Description of Ireland (1610)
Seymour, St. John – Irish Witchcraft and Demonology (1913)
Summers, Montagu – History of Witchcraft and Demonology
Yeats, W. B. – Irish Fairy and Folk Tales

ALSO BY PATRICK F. BYRNE

IRISH GHOST STORIES 75 p

There is a strong and ancient tradition of ghosts in Ireland. While many of the tales are obvious figments of imagination, there are certain stories which cannot be explained away.

The author has probed deeply into many of these spooky goings-on in all parts of the country, and relates his findings here.

Perhaps the most horrifying stories refer to the 'Hungry Grass', a product of the unspeakable horror left in people's minds by the Famine. It grows where a victim of the Famine perished; and to cross it at night is to be seized with a hunger which causes death if not immediately satisfied.

OTHER MERCIER PAPERBACKS

THE HORSE THIEVES OF BALLYSAGGERT 30P
Brian Cleeve

A selection of short stories by the well-known Irish T.V. personality. The stories are unusual in theme, and make compelling reading.

THE COMIC HISTORY OF IRELAND 55P
E. J. Delaney & J. M. Feehan

Our history may well have been sad, but this hilarious, irrepressible giggle-maker lifts the gloom right off our backs.

THE CELTS 65 p
edited by Joseph Raftery

A selection of essays on the various Celtic traditions, the languages, the classical authors, Celtic religion and society.

FOLKLORE BY KEVIN DANAHER

IN IRELAND LONG AGO 50P

The author gives a fascinating picture of old Ireland through his wide knowledge of Irish rural life and tradition.

GENTLE PLACES AND SIMPLE THINGS 50P

More tales of Irish life for all who would like to know how our people lived, loved and were entertained before the traditional way of life was destroyed.

IRISH COUNTRY PEOPLE 50P

Here Kevin Danaher gives interesting and appealing pictures of the almost-forgotten people of Ireland – the tailor, the mason, the blacksmith, the basket-maker, and the currach-maker.

FOLKTALES OF THE IRISH COUNTRYSIDE 75p

Send us your name + address if you would like to receive regular news of Mercier books.

www.mercierpress.ie

www.ingramcontent.com/pod-product-compliance
Lightning Source LLC
Chambersburg PA
CBHW070059100426
42743CB00012B/2597